CONTENTS:

INTRODUCTION
BILL GETHING

More than almost any other aspect of our current lifestyle, the link between transportation and carbon dioxide emissions from burning fossil fuels could not be clearer. Where else is the compactness and potency of the ancient sunlight stored as fossil fuel so essential as in its use for transportation; particularly so for air travel and the free form personal road based transportation system on which our current lifestyle is based.

The pincer movement of ever rising emissions and ever reducing "safe" limits for atmospheric CO_2 concentrations has generated an increasing sense of urgency in rising to the challenge of climate change.

This has been reflected in a tightening of targets such as the United Kingdom (UK) government's 60 per cent reduction in CO_2 emissions by 2050, as set out in the 2003 Energy White Paper, which is to be interrogated by the new Committee on Climate Change, with every likelihood that it will be increased; perhaps to 80 per cent.

There is a growing frustration with long term targets such as these in that they appear irrelevant to decisions that need to be made today. However, they are useful in defining the order of magnitude of the overall challenge ahead and set a more radical agenda than simply assuming that the necessary change can be achieved by incremental improvement. Rather than think about how to cut 80 per cent of our emissions, it may be more constructive to consider how to use the 20 per cent most effectively in achieving a genuinely sustainable lifestyle. Clearly, our transport habits and systems will need to be very different in this context. The challenge, of course, is to plan an orderly transition from our current situation to that sustainable future, making best use of the existing networks and technologies available to us. To take a building analogy, this must be a conversion, not a new build project.

The Mayor of London's Climate Change Action Plan has adopted a shorter timeframe; setting a target of a 60 per cent reduction by 2025 that relates conveniently to the time span of this series of these Edge commentaries.[1] Breaking this target down still further implies something of the order of a ten per cent reduction by 2010 (just two years away…) and something of the order of 40 per cent reduction by 2015, given that we will sensibly take advantage of relatively easy wins by reducing waste in the system as soon as possible and that reductions will progressively become more difficult. The urgency of making demonstrable and immediate progress in reversing the seemingly unstoppable trends of increasing emissions is made abundantly clear when set in these timeframes.

1 *Action Today to Protect Tomorrow— The Mayor's Climate Change Action Plan*, London: GLA, February 2007

The government is in the process of producing transportation strategies and consultation programmes and these are reviewed in some detail by Hank Dittmar. However, it feels that the primary focus of these strategies and the reports that support them, however authoritative, betrays the dangers of trying to deal with the transition to a low carbon lifestyle in a piecemeal way. The Eddington Transport Study, for example, takes as its fundamental principle that "transport's key role now is supporting the success of the UK's highly productive urban areas in the global market place and enabling efficient movement of goods". Climate change is referred to but only in the context of noting that "transport prices must fully reflect environmental externalities, and transport planning must take account of likely carbon prices".[2]

2 *Eddington Transport Study Executive Summary,* Department for Transport, October 2007, p. 11

In setting out its agenda in this way, the report immediately limits the primary contribution that transport can make to a more sustainable lifestyle to improving the efficiency of the system rather than the far greater impact that a coordinated approach to planning and transport could make on overall sustainability or carbon efficiency. The integration of land use, density requirements and transportation planning, arguably the most powerful combination of tools for sustainable planning, is excluded as being outside the scope of the study—although it is acknowledged that: "Where there is significant new development, then it will be important for transport and land use to be developed together."[3]

3 *Eddington Transport Study Executive Summary,* Department for Transport, October 2007, p. 45

Similarly, the Department for Transport's discussion paper: *Towards a Sustainable Transport System*, whilst it refers to the importance of a local role for encouraging modal shifts and reducing people's need to travel, its fundamental thrust is belied by its sub-title: *Supporting Economic Growth in a Low Carbon World*.[4] Surely a more balanced approach is needed using the full range of available

4 *Towards a Sustainable Transport System,* Department for Transport, 2007

planning tools in a coordinated way to deal with the new challenges that face us. Would it be too much to hope that the next DfT strategy paper might be entitled: "The Role for Transport Systems in Supporting a Sustainable Low Carbon Lifestyle?"

Fundamentally, there are limited options available to us to reduce transport emissions:

- To reduce the amount or fossil fuelled travel

- To use fossil fuels more efficiently—by using more efficient modes of transport, developing more efficient engines and vehicles and modifying driving behaviour (according to the Mayor of London's Climate Change Action Plan, five to ten per cent savings could be achieved by the latter alone!)

- To develop alternative low or zero carbon transport fuels (without adversely affecting other essential aspects of our collective lifestyle—for example competing with food production in terms of affordability or availability)

Of course it is possible that a technological magic bullet might emerge that would enable us to carry on exactly as we are. To rely on this would not only demonstrate an excessive faith in technology but also miss the opportunity to review the way we organise our lives to see if the challenge suggests ways to improve our quality of life without significantly reducing economic prosperity.

Given our addiction to cheap, easy travel, our immediate reaction to the concept of travelling less is to see this as a restriction rather than a benefit. However, for example, reducing the distance and time between the workplace and the home offers the possibility of improving our work/life balance, as well as improving our health and fitness and the social cohesion of our currently fragmented communities once they are transformed from sterile dormitories into animated neighbourhoods that are accessible by walking and cycling.

Improving communication technologies offer the potential for more sophisticated and responsive approaches to demand-led shared transport, more efficient alternatives to routine shopping, electronic alternatives to business travel for meetings, etc., and for mobile working as an alternative to location specific workplaces. Of course some of the "opportunities" which we currently take for granted may be less available: access to cheap holiday destinations in far off places, some limitation in the choice of work available or the opportunities of experiencing the wider world. Even the most sophisticated electronic technologies are limited in their ability (at present) to transfer the essence (the smells, the character, the culture and the atmosphere) of exotic locations down a wire.

Reduction in some apparent freedoms and limiting choice through measures such as congestion charging or prioritising road use for public transport may, at first sight, appear restricting to the individual but could reap significant collective benefits which will in turn result in individual benefits.

It is clear is that we need radically to change the way we behave, individually and collectively. In order to make the change we need a financial and legislative framework that encourages and, if necessary, compels us to do so. It is a key responsibility for our elected representatives to set that framework: prioritising the use of limited resources (or, in the current circumstances, prioritising the right to pollute) for the common good. Key to the framework will be a mechanism the redress the failure of the market to reflect the true cost of carbon as noted in *The Stern Review* in

October 2006. This fundamental issue has been reiterated in all the strategies and government reports that have followed it, however, as yet the government has been silent on what form this will take.

However, we also need a collective vision (or visions) of a different and desirable way of life that we can all sign up to. Without this it will not be possible to guarantee the political mandate for the consistent long term policies that will be essential in making the transition to our low carbon future.

This book offers one such vision of life in 2025, setting it in the context of our current transport systems and policies. It is supported by a current case study that illustrates a range of analytical and consultation tools that can be used in devising a shared approach to the master planning of a town centre. It demonstrates how, in a relatively contained urban situation, the complex interrelationships between transport, density, social and economic issues can be understood in sufficient detail to allow a genuinely holistic approach to devising such a vision. It concludes by outlining some of the pitfalls of current strategies and some pointers towards the kind of comprehensive policies that will be necessary to tackle the challenges ahead.

The need to change is clear. What is considerably less clear is the event or set of circumstances that will convince us to change the habits of the past 100 or so years in time to make the transition to a low carbon future anything other than messy and painful. If we are worthy of the name of our species, Homo Sapiens, we will be able to use our intelligence to make an ordered transition into a different phase of our development, building on the platform that abundant cheap energy has given us. However, if we simply rely on our more basic instincts and ignore the mounting challenges of the future, we can only expect a future that will indeed be lower carbon, but simply as a result of a chaotic breakdown of a redundant industrial society.

A VISION FOR TRANSPORT AND NEIGHBOURHOODS IN 2025
HANK DITTMAR

The Seymour Household, Peterborough, An Average Day in 2025

Nigel and Sally woke to the gentle sound of the house waking itself and everybody inside with the approach of the new day. Coffee was brewing, lively pop music was playing upstairs on the children's floor, and the *Today Programme* was murmuring in the background. It was an office day for Sally, and while she enjoyed the chance to see colleagues once a week, she groaned as she thought about selecting a smart suit to wear. Nigel was the cheery one in the morning, and he hummed as he slipped into a pair of jeans and a shirt to walk the children to school.

Upstairs Ben and Andy were squabbling as usual, in that affectionate yet irritated tone that twins often seem to adopt. While they looked forward to each day at the Academy, it wasn't on to let the parents or each other know that, and so they complained as they got ready. Downstairs, Nigel found fresh milk, bread and eggs on the doorstep, delivered from the local shop by pedi-cab each morning. After a hurried breakfast together, the family all left the house, with Sally rushing to catch the tram and Nigel and the boys walking the ten minutes to school.

Sally's guided bus trip to the station was uneventful. It was standing room only, but for a ride of less than 15 minutes, that wasn't a problem. She hurried to the platform to catch the express to London on the Main Line. It cost a bit more to take the high-speed but the 30 minute journey time made it well worth the expense. The 200 mile per hour trains were showing their age, having been introduced in 2015, but replacement train sets were supposedly being introduced next year, reducing the journey time to 20 minutes. It wasn't so bad, as she only had to endure the commute once a week on office days. She had time for a cup of tea before the train pulled into King's Cross, and then she had to jump a tram down to the City.

Nigel and the boys walked through the light drizzle to the school, which was located at the neighbourhood centre next to theirs. After saying good-bye at the playground, Nigel stopped in at the neighbourhood clinic, located in the same complex, for his physical therapy session. Back at the house, Nigel stepped out back to the studio at the back of their garden. When they had bought the house, they had considered the live-work option, with ground floor office and house upstairs, but had opted for the separate studio space in the back. Nigel sometimes saw clients at home and he preferred them to enter through the mews door. And the small apartment upstairs generated some extra income. His CAD technician was just logging into the office system, and Nigel stopped to look at the changes his partner in Mumbai had made to the plans overnight. They had a design review that morning with the client.

Sally's tram ride to her office off Holborn was quick as London's congestion charge had been succeeded by the controversial central London peak period personal car ban in 2020. The trams automatically triggered the signals, and took precedence over the black taxis, electric scooter and tricycles and bicycles that now ruled London's streets.

Ben and Andy's school day included a virtual lecture by one of the curators at The British Museum. They'd been studying Egypt that week, and so it was wicked to see and smell the musty odour of the mummies through the Virtual Reality (VR) kit. After lunch it was a sports day, and they enjoyed the track and field competition. Nigel met them at the end of the school day, and they walked together to the park at the edge of their neighbourhood for the twins footie practice. Nigel took the opportunity to put in a good 40 minutes pulling weeds in the family's allotment nearby. He picked some rocket and some early peas for dinner. On the way home they stopped at the butchers for some sausages as well.

The twins were finishing their homework on the computer when Sally returned from work. She'd worked late and had to settle for warmed up dinner, but the family joined her for pudding and hot chocolate. Over their drinks they discussed the plans for their summer holiday. The children wanted to go back to Newquay for a week on the beach, but Nigel favoured a high-speed train trip to the south of France, pointing out the carbon allotment for the very efficient high-speed train was only a little greater than the older trains to the Southwest. In the end Sally voted with the children for surfing in Cornwall.

After quick baths, the children got to bed. Nigel had a late video conference call with his partner Vivendra in Mumbai, to go over the decisions reached in the meeting with the client, and discuss where he'd left the design by the end of the day. They hoped to have the next submission ready for review by the end of the workday in India. While Nigel was on the call, Sally did the carbon tallies for the last month, and authorised the electronic payment from their account. They were well within their budget for the month, and in fact were on track for a rebate from their energy coop if they didn't blow the budget with holiday travel, or through overuse of household appliances.

Sally and Nigel signed off their respective computers and were off to bed, as the house automatically powered down for the night.

How we got there
A low carbon day in 2025 will be much like a high carbon day in 2008. Technology will have incrementally improved, and cleaner technologies are in much wider use than in 2008, but there hasn't been a technological breakthrough or radical change, except in the way we behave. And the way we behave hasn't changed that much: families still squabble, people still grumble abut overcrowded trains and still skate too close to the edge with household budgets—and they look for ways to beat the system. What has changed is that people are willing to change: prompted by an economic system that makes wasting energy personally expensive and a set of convenient and pleasurable green choices.

The collapse of the truckers and farmers protests in 2009, coupled with a growing awareness in the business community that responding to the environmental crisis could be profitable, led to a braver politicians. By 2009 government realised that it couldn't have its cake and eat it too; that a strong carbon credit and charging system had to be accompanied by an effort to link planning and development choices with investment in greener transport and energy infrastructure. The Queen's Speech in 2009 proposed the first post-carbon budget for the UK, and this time it was clear that the government had decided to stick with it, no matter the consequences. Once it was clear that the party in power wasn't going to back down the other parties came along as well, and the carbon charging and national road pricing programmes were adopted.

Household and corporate carbon budgets were widely adopted and the new Accounting for Sustainability corporate reporting standards were a required part of all annual statements across the public, private and NGO sectors.

On the planning and development side, it became illegal to build an urban or suburban house more than 400 metres from a bus stop with frequent service. All new growth allocations were accompanied with an assessment against land value for the construction of green infrastructure: trams, rapid buses, bikeways and interchange improvements, as well as renewable energy and sustainable drainage and along with an increase in density to make the infrastructure feasible. New cost benefit analyses for local transport schemes factored in developer contributions to local and regional public transport as well as fully accounting for avoided emissions, and the principle of the mixed-use walkable neighbourhood as the core of the accessible region became not just policy but practice.

Ubiquitous smart card technology allowed for time of day congestion charging in all the major cities, with the funds used to match developer contributions for green transport schemes for public transport, walking and cycling. Home-based work flourished as a result, and it became popular for business to offer employment packages for such work, with one or two days per week in the office, and the rest worked at home or in satellite work centres which sprang up in bookshops and cafes across the country. Employers offered incentive programmes with banks and building societies for the conversion of garages and lofts into accessory units and workspaces to encourage the trend, and empty upper storey space above retail was converted to flats, reducing the need for new construction.

The opening of the high-speed service into St Pancras Station opened up the eyes of many in the UK to the progress that had been made on the Continent in the provision of high quality, high-speed intercity rail service, and the evident economic benefits for business travellers became evident as well. The overall quality and attention to consumer experience contrasted sharply with high prices, overcrowding and unreliability in the British rail system, and a popular consensus began to demand improvements in service. The Trans-British Networks were announced as a complement to the Trans European Networks in the 2009 message as well, with a new high-speed alignment north, as well as high-speed service to Cardiff from London. Copying the example of Swiss Rail, high-speed trains now run on the half hour and hour in every major British city.

The advent of the aviation carbon charging scheme and the individual carbon budget sounded the death knell for cheap air travel, and as high-speed rail across the Continent and within the British Isles became more prevalent, there was a mode shift for journeys under three hours. Video conferencing was increasingly used for business meetings and families began to take holidays closer to home.

From the perspective of 2025, it is hard to see that it could have ended up any other way. Change was necessary, and humans have always adjusted. Many of the changes feared in 2008 ended up adding to our quality of life here in the UK, and in fact we eat better, are healthier and have just as many choices as those turn of the century people: they are just different choices!

THE VIEW FROM HERE:
TRANSPORT TODAY

The daily life of the fictional Seymour
family in 2025 contrasts sharply with the
average British household experience
with transport and commuting in 2008,
although the seeds of the transformation
may have already been planted.

In present day UK, the average family's
transport and energy consumption is
among the highest in the world, behind
that of the United States and Australia,
but ahead of most other countries.

In 2006, there were 33.7 million licensed
drivers in the UK, and 33.4 million
licensed motor vehicles. For many
decades, transportation analysts warned
of the economic impact of the saturation
of the domestic auto market as the ratio
of drivers to cars neared one to one.

But the nation has already reached the supposed saturation point, and the number of vehicles owned has continued to grow steadily—by 70 per cent between 1980 and 2006.

Now cars are seen as lifestyle objects, and many of us appear to require multiple vehicles for our many faceted lives. In 2005, 75 per cent of all households had access to at least one car, and 25 per cent of all households had access to at least two cars. The wealthier a household is the more vehicles it owns.

During the last 25 years, the country has experienced a continued explosion in car use, particularly in the 1980s, when car traffic grew from 215 million vehicle kilometres travelled to over 300 million. Growth in driving slowed after 1990, but between 1980 and 2006, car use grew by 87 per cent, from 215 million vehicle kilometres to 402 million kilometres. There was a drop in travel in 2004–2005, but between 2005 and 2006, car traffic grew again.

Transport is a growing part of the climate change problem. As emissions from other sectors of the economy have declined in recent years, transport's carbon emissions have continued to grow from 14 per cent of the UK's CO_2 emissions in 1980 to 23 per cent by 1997. According to the UK's Environmental Accounts, household use of private vehicles accounted for 40 per cent of greenhouse gas emissions in the transport sector in 2005, having seen a 12 per cent increase since 1990. Road freight transport emissions have grown by 38 per cent over the same period.

Automobile by-products including brake and tyre particulates, air toxins and pollutants and road chemicals, run off into groundwater and are increasingly acknowledged as a major source of both ground and surface water pollution. And impervious surfaces prevent rainwater from percolating into groundwater, leading to increased levels of runoff into canalised river systems, and increasing flooding risk.

Although the number of people killed or seriously injured in road accidents has declined significantly since 1980, due primarily to safer vehicles, 31,845 people were killed or seriously injured in the UK in 2006.

The recent UK *Foresight Tackling Obesities: Future Choices* report by the Government Office for Science and Technology looked at the alarming rise in the incidence of obesities in the UK, concluding that by 2050 60 per cent of adult men, 50 per cent of adult women and about 25 per cent of all children under 16 could be obese, leading to increased chronic disease risk from diabetes, stroke and coronary disease and economic costs to society and business of over £49 billion in today's currency. The report concluded:

> human biology is being overwhelmed by the effects of today's obese-ogenic environment, with its abundance of energy dense food, motorised transport and sedentary lifestyles.[5]

Indeed, although doctors recommend 30 minutes of moderate physical activity per day, the actual amount of time Britons spend walking and cycling has declined from 12.9 minutes in 1995–1996 to 11.8 minutes in 2005–2006, a decrease of eight per cent in just a decade. The *Foresight* report concluded that there might be a win-win solution:

> Many climate change goals would also help prevent obesity, such as measures to reduce traffic congestion, increase cycling or design sustainable communities.[6]

5 *UK Foresight Programme Tackling Obesities: Future Choices*, The Government Office for Science and Technology, 2007, summary, p. 2

6 *UK Foresight Programme Tackling Obesities: Future Choices*, p. 5

Signs of Change

All is not gloom and doom, however. In the past decade it is possible to see that progress has been made in dealing with the social and environmental impacts of our transportation system, and doing so in a way that delivers economic benefits. While the overall trends may not yet be positive government urban policy has begun to realign around sustainable new communities; London has led the way in shifting consumers toward public transport, walking and cycling; there is a Europe wide trend toward increased intercity passenger rail travel; and there is some evidence of a decoupling of economic growth from its long relationship with growth in travel by car.

Changing Urban Policy

A number of forces came together in the 1990s to bring about a change in government policy toward new development: the success of the Prince of Wales' development at Poundbury and the growing influence of the Urban Villages Forum sponsored by Business in the Community, the report from the Urban Task Force by Lord Richard Rogers of Riverside, and the growing influence of the New Urbanism, a US-based design movement championed here by former Deputy Prime Minister John Prescott.[7] All of these diverse forces promoted a return to many of the design attributes of the traditional city, and away from the car dominated, functionally separated model encouraged by government in the post-war period. The diagram on the next page graphically depicts the two development and road network paradigms.

7 Towards an Urban Renaissance: Final Report of the Urban Task Force, London: E&FN Spon, 1999

The differences can be characterised in this way:

- The suburban model relies upon physical separation of differing uses—houses, shops, schools and workplaces—into separate zones, and uses a road network based upon cul-de-sacs and channelling through traffic onto a limited set of higher capacity routes. This increases distances between activities and forces reliance upon the motor vehicle for most trips. Buildings are separated by parking lots and the streets are faced with parking, further disadvantaging the pedestrian and cyclist.

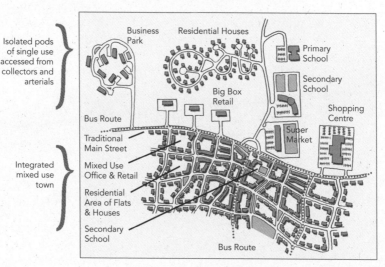

Contemporary Suburban Model

Isolated pods of single use accessed from collectors and arterials

Business Park

Residential Houses

Primary School

Secondary School

Big Box Retail

Shopping Centre

Bus Route

Traditional Main Street

Integrated mixed use town

Mixed Use Office & Retail

Residential Area of Flats & Houses

Secondary School

Super Market

Bus Route

Sustainable Urbanism

- Sustainable urbanism rejects the notion of segregating uses and instead mixes housing, shops, schools and workplaces into what is called the walkable neighbourhood—with shops and higher density activities on the main street and all uses interconnected by a permeable and walkable street network. Daily needs should be accessible within a five-minute walk.

These principles have been enshrined into government policy through Planning Policy Guidance, and are increasingly imbedded into standards such as those promoted by the Commission for Architecture and the Built Environment and sustainability checklists developed by the Building Research Establishment with several of England's Regional Development Agencies.

Pioneering projects such as Poundbury, the Prince of Wales' own development with the Duchy of Cornwall in Dorset, which will accommodate 5,000 people, and already has 700 people working and 1,200 people living there, have shown that mixed-use, mixed-income developments centred on walkable neighburhoods can succeed in the marketplace. Poundbury challenged conventional paradigms for street design, reducing widths and sight distance, eliminating road signs and forcing drivers to respond to the urban environment rather than tailoring the urban environment solely for the car. Its innovations and similar efforts by English Partnerships with The Prince's Foundation at Upton and elsewhere, have informed the Department for Transport's new *Manual for Streets*, which incorporates many of these ideas.[8]

8 *Manual for Streets*, Department for Transport, March 2007

A step beyond the notion of the reintroduction of the walkable street network is the idea of public transport orientated development, which argues for concentrating new development around new railway or tram stops. London's Passenger Transport Accessibility Level (PTAL) approach to allocating housing near areas of high public transport accessibility reflects many of these ideas. Guidelines for transport-orientated development have been developed by myself and colleagues in a US-focused publication called *New Transit Town*.[9] This 2004 book documents the boom in construction of new tram, rapid bus and commuter railway systems in the US. 37 of the 40 largest cities are building new railway services at the present time—as a framework for accommodating metropolitan area growth. Voters in Dallas, Texas, Denver, Colorado and Charlotte, North Carolina have all voted to tax themselves to build new rail and guided

9. Dittmar, Hank and Gloria Ohland, *New Transit Town*, Washington, DC: Island Press, 2004

Streets at Poundbury in Dorset (Photos: Richard Ivey for the Prince's Foundation)

bus systems to create highly accessible green networks to structure regional growth. In this country, the Northstowe "eco-town" outside Cambridge, promoted by English Partnerships and designed by Arup, is aligned around a rapid bus system, as is the Sherford New Community, designed by The Prince's Foundation and Paul Murrain. Sherford, an extension to Plymouth on the edge of the South Hams, will eventually accommodate 5,500 affordable and market rate homes, a traditional high street and employment within four walkable neighbourhoods. An analysis of accessibility ensured that daily needs could be accessed within a five minute walk, many other needs within a ten minute walk, and other activities could be accessed by rapid, convenient public transport. It is organised around green infrastructure including sustainable urban drainage, green corridors to a county park which include flyways for bats, a serious commitment to renewable energy and energy conservation in building, and local sourcing and food strategies. Sherford will be built according to a town code, ensuring that the streets will remain walkable, build quality will be high and master-plan commitments will be followed.

A significant opportunity for such public transport orientated development also exists at the Ebbsfleet Channel Tunnel Rail Link station, both around the station and at the adjacent Eastern Quarry development. The potential for transport orientated development is hindered, however, by the lack of financing tools for constructing this kind of new infrastructure at the local or regional level and the reluctance of central government to consider anything other than narrow cost-benefit criteria related to travel when assessing new transport projects.

A Look at London
London has been in the forefront of cities dealing with sustainable transportation globally, largely due to former Mayor Ken Livingstone's leadership in proposing congestion pricing, and in using the funds generated by pricing to improve London's bus services. At the same time, London has England's most widespread and accessible public transport, its areas of greatest density and a street network that precedes the development of the suburban cul-de-sac system.

One only needs to compare the share of total trips by public transport in London with other British cities to learn that Greater London is starting from a much higher base. In the UK as a whole, two thirds (64 per cent) of all trips are taken by car, as compared to London, where less than half of all trips (43 per cent) are made by car.

For Central London, the public transport share is even greater, with only nine per cent of work trips to Central London being made by car, despite the fact that Central London work journeys continue to increase. In fact, the number of people entering Central London by car has fallen by 40 per cent since 1995, while bus journeys have increased by 83 per cent. Rail use in London has increased as well, particularly light rail use, which has grown five-fold with the introduction of the Croydon tram and extensions to the Docklands light railway.[10]

Bus use has been declining in most regions across the UK even as this turnaround in bus travel in London has occurred. According to the Department for Transport, most regions have seen a decline in bus patronage, while service kilometres have remained steady over the last decade. The number of households within 15 minutes of public transport service has declined over the last decade in a majority of British regions as well.

The answer to London's surprising success in increasing bus and rail use seems to be simple: the congestion charging scheme has depressed car travel into Central London and generated revenue which has allowed an increase in the provision of public transport services, as well as improvement in cycling and pedestrian accessibility. At the same time, authority for major roads, public transport service levels and policy has been devolved, with this funding capacity, to the Greater London Authority. The London Plan has pushed up densities and pushed down provision of car parking, as public transport provision has increased. As a result, the utility of the public

10 National Statistics and Department for Transport, Regional Transport Statistics, 2006 Edition, p. 15

transport and its accessibility have increased and users of the road network have begun to pay something closer to the full costs of private transport by car.

The devolution of similar authority and funding capacity for public transport to the metropolitan scale across the UK is a hotly debated topic, but at this time improvements in public transport service are rare outside London, as the government is slow to invest in rail or tram projects, and bus services are run by competitive private companies with little incentive to improve overall accessibility or cooperate with local authorities. The ideology of privatisation has penetrated deeply into the public transport sector, and the public utility aspect has declined with overall accessibility levels in most British regions.

Trans-European Networks: A Revival of Rail Travel

The long awaited arrival of the first Paris train into St Pancras Station in London awakened many to the renaissance in high-speed high-quality passenger rail service on the European Continent. High-speed rail service has become a feature of daily life in London over the past decade with Germany's ICE trains, the Thalys service from Paris to Brussels and Amsterdam and high-speed Spanish services joining France's famous—and growing—TGV network. This expending network is reducing journey times and improving connections all over Europe, and it is coming about as a result of European Union policy to designate Trans-European networks.

The use of passenger rail has been growing across the European Union, but the UK rail patronage per inhabitant lags behind that of other leading European nations. Germans travel 865 rail passenger-kilometres per inhabitant each year, the French travel 1,231 rail passenger-kilometres per person annually, while the average the UK resident travels only 674 rail passenger-kilometres per annum. The average of EU-nations surveyed is 812 passenger-kilometres per annum. It should be noted that rail travel per capita in the UK is growing, from 592 passenger-kilometres in 1997 to 674 in 2002, a 14 per cent increase.[11]

11 Eurostat,
Energy, Transport
and Environment
Indicators, 2005
Edition, p. 120

Key

1 - Secondary School
2 - Primary School
3 - Health Centre & Children's Centre
4 - Sports Centre
5 - Youth Centre
6 - High Street
7 - Community Park
8 - Outdoor Sports Facilities

9 - Wildlife and Green corridors
10 - Sherford quarry (disused)
11 - Existing woodlands
12 - Existing farm houses and buildings
13 - Park and Ride interchange
14 - Key Feature Building
15 - King George V playing fields
16 - Community Wind Turbines

Project

SHERFORD

ILLUSTRATIVE
TOWN PLAN

Drawing title		Scale size 1:5000 @ A1	0 25 50 100 m	The Prince's Foundation	
		Drawn DP/IM/TY	Checked SG	19-22 Charlotte Road London, EC2A 3SG Tel: 0207 613 8500 Fax: 0207 613 8599 enquiry@princes-foundation.org www.princes-foundation.org	The Prince's Foundation FOR THE BUILT ENVIRONMENT
		Client REDTREE	Date 09.11.2006		
		THIS DRAWING MAY BE USED ONLY FOR THE PURPOSE INTENDED AND ONLY WRITTEN DIMENSIONS SHALL BE USED		Drawing number 038-III/11.1001	Rev OPA

The increase in inter-city rail travel is the result of efforts to improve services, and the extent of high-speed service on the continent is striking, especially when compared to the UK. New high-speed trains on new or comprehensively improved alignments are common, as are improvements in capacity and running times for regional services. In 2007, Europe's high-speed rail operators joined together in a programme called "RailTeam" to promote interoperability and to promote the network as a European network. The only portion of the British rail network participating is the link from Paris to London, as the RailTeam map shows.

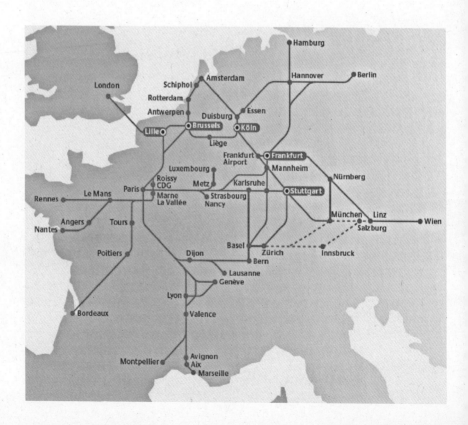

The government published its white paper *Toward a Sustainable Transport System* in July 2007, some months before their transport proposals. The report counsels against moving toward high-speed services before 2014, arguing that consumers value reliability over speed. Instead the government proposes increases in train and platform length to accommodate more passengers, and suggests that major plans to improve infrastructure be deferred until the future is more clear, perhaps after 2014, arguing that:

> it would not be prudent to commit now to 'all-or-nothing' projects, such as network-wide electrification or a high-speed line, for which the longer-term benefits are currently uncertain and which could delay tackling the current strategic priorities such as capacity.[12]

12 *Toward a Sustainable Transport System*, Department for Transport, July 2007, p. 11

While it is clear that improving the performance and capacity of existing services is critical—and network performance is vital as Railtrack cause over half of all delays—achieving a step change in rail use and a shift from short distance air travel and car use to rail travel will necessitate integrated thinking and planning.

The trend is clearly toward rail travel, as the government acknowledges: "Rail has seen demand grow by 40 per cent in the last ten years, and a further 30 per cent growth is projected for the next ten years on the base scenario. Taking the two decades together, demand will have grown by over 80 per cent. In fact, in the last decade the rail system has regained all of the passengers it lost in the 40 years since Beeching's cuts to the rail network in the 1960s. Early in 2008, it was announced that rail travel in England had reached an all time high. It is interesting that this increase in rail travel has happened in a period when the costs of motoring have declined in real terms and the costs of rail travel have increased by over 40 per cent.

While the government defers spending and even planning until the future becomes clear, governments all over the world are investing in major improvements to railway services.

THE TRANSPORT POLICY LANDSCAPE

The gap between the present and our vision for 2025 will only be closed by policy reforms, and this Chapter seeks to assess recent progress in making the profound shifts in policy required to get to a low carbon networked transport future. Much of the research background is in place, and many of the policies as well, but there remains a fundamental disconnect between high-level policy and practice. A look at four recent policy documents reveals how muddled our thinking is about sustainable communities and transport.

The Stern Review: The Economics of Climate Change

Perhaps the most influential review in the past few years has been Sir Nicholas Stern's report on climate change and the economy. *The Stern Review* had a major impact on thinking abut climate change for it lodged two arguments: first, that the economic consequences of failing to act quickly with respect to climate change would be disastrous, but secondly that acting quickly could lead to positive economic returns. Stern argued for a mix of actions: the introduction of carbon markets to set a price for carbon, technology introduction, but also the removal of barriers to effective implementation. In particular Stern cited the need for regulation, better information and financing.

Stern pointed out that market imperfections created major obstacles to the implementation of mitigation measures, and noted that individuals and firms do not always act to make the most cost-effective decisions and choices. In particular he cited the need for improved building regulation, advice the government has already taken to heart, with the commitment to zero carbon homes by 2016. With respect to transport and development, *The Stern Review* notes that:

> Spatial and strategic planning can affect patterns of energy consumption. Higher density urban environments, for example, typically consume less energy for transport and in buildings. In addition, land use controls such as restrictions on the availability and pricing of parking spaces, the use of pedestrian zones and parks and land use zonal strategies (including congestion charging), have the potential to support integrated public transport to reduce the use of private motor vehicles.[13]

13 Stern, Nicholas, *The Economics of Climate Change*, The Stern Review, Cambridge: Cambridge University Press, 2001, p. 384

Stern thus calls for actions to "promote efficiency through strategic coordination of key markets, for example by reducing long-run transport demand through integrated land-use planning and infrastructure development."[14]

14 Stern Review, 2006, p. 381

The Barker Review of Land Use Planning

Hard on the heels of Sir Nicholas Stern's review of the economics of climate change came economist Kate Barker's review of land use planning and the market, issued in December 2006. *The Barker Review* examined the role of the planning system and recommended a number of steps aimed at improving its efficiency, transparency and using it to deliver 'sustainable economic objectives'. Early on in the report Barker notes: "planning plays a role in the mitigation of and adaptation to climate change, the biggest issue faced across all climate areas."[15] Barker's report proposes that rather than local authorities being responsible for determining whether there is a need for a proposed development, developers merely need to demonstrate there is demand for the development, effectively reversing the presumption inherent in British planning law since the passage of the Town and Country Planning Act in 1948.

15 *Barker Review* of Land Use Planning, Department of Communities and Local Governments, 2006, p.3

As soon as Barker brings up climate adaptation and mitigation, however, she dismisses it as irrelevant, except for speeding the permitting of renewable energy installations. In a direct conflict with *The Stern Review*, *The Barker Review* concludes that:

> In this context it is important that the planning system not be asked to bear a disproportionate weight of the overall approach to this issue. In terms of transport emissions, for example, the evidence on the link between urban form and emissions is complex and contested, while planning often influences behaviour, requiring a site to be accessed by public transport does not mean that it will in fact be accessed that way.... Pricing mechanisms, on the other hand, could result in widespread behavioural change even in the short term, and do so in a direct way by altering incentives. They may therefore be more efficient and effective tools for mitigating climate change impact.[16]

16 *Barker Review*, p. 34

Stern argues for a mutually reinforcing and holistic regime that backs pricing signals and technology introduction with regulation, better information to aid market decisions and financing. Barker prefers to rely on market signals alone and dismisses applying the Stern proposals to the planning systems. With respect to Stern's proposal for coordination of planning with infrastructure investment, by directing growth to areas where public transport investment is planned—he cites the Chinese example of Dongtan—Barker merely cites the need for expedited approval of major transport schemes through an independent commission.

The Eddington Transport Study

Sir Rod Eddington's review of transport's role in sustaining the UK's productivity and competitiveness was released in 2007, and seeks to underpin the government's approach to delivering a sustainable transport system. Eddington unabashedly puts competitiveness and productivity at the top of the sustainability pyramid, reducing the environment and social dimensions to secondary roles. He concludes that the UK transport system "provides the right connections, in the right places, to support the journeys that matter in terms of economic performance".[17]

17 *Eddington Transport Study*, HM Treasury and Department for Transport, 2007, p. 3

Eddington approvingly cites *The Stern Review*, and indeed Sir Nicholas Stern chaired the Academic Friends group convened to assist Sir Rod Eddington with the report. In the context of the environment, Eddington proposes that all environmental costs and benefits be analysed in making transport decisions, and the report attempts to develop a framework for doing so that reviews available policy choices.

Eddington focused upon improving the performance of the existing system, rather than building major new infrastructure, based on rate of return on investment measures across a series of studies of major schemes. He favours targeted infrastructure investment where high returns can be demonstrated, and emphasises congestion mitigation rather than new connections. Notably exempted from Eddington's critique of big projects—which seem mainly to refer to rail and urban public transport schemes— are a number of trunk road improvements and investments in airport and port infrastructure.

The report tends to favour small projects over large ones, noting with EF Schumacher that "small is beautiful", and suggests that projects focused upon walking and cycling can deliver positive returns due to their environmental benefits. Along with Barker, Eddington proposes a national Independent Planning Commission to expedite decisions on major projects.

In looking at the relationship between transport and the economy, Eddington puts it simply:

> the relationship between transport demand and GDP growth in the post-war years, illustrates clearly the very close relationship between transport and growth.[18]

18 *Eddington Study*, p. 14

Eddington notes, however, that these historic relationships were largely driven by the provision of the system—and I would argue by the shift toward personal automobile travel—and that as the system matures, complex microeconomic drivers come into play. These include increased need for reliability due to just-in-time logistics, the role of urban transport in supporting agglomeration, and the role of transport in supporting international trade. I will argue later that these enable us to decouple GDP from increased use of the transport system, and that it is possible to improve the economy without increasing Vehicle Kilometres Travelled.

Eddington's view that environment and social factors are externalities rather than core pillars of a sustainable society colours his approach, however, for he never addresses the need to fundamentally increase the mode shares for the greener modes of rail, subway, bus, walking and cycling. And while Eddington proposes that the government ought to direct new housing to areas of existing transport capacity, he never proposes a more strategic approach that would increase public transport capacity in order to facilitate increased development where it can be accommodated in a sustainable manner. For Eddington, try as he might to shed it, is still locked in the model of transport responding to demand generated by the economy. For example, he views road pricing principally as a tool for dealing with congestion, arguing that from a congestion perspective, a national system needs to be in place by 2015, but doesn't address its value in actually reflecting environmental costs and creating a mode shift to public transport.

19 *Towards a Sustainable Transport System*, Department for Transport, 2007

Towards a Sustainable Transport System[19]

In October 2007, Secretary of State for Transport Ruth Kelly introduced the government's response to *The Eddington Study* and *The Stern Review*. With respect to Stern, the submission to Parliament points out that Stern has demonstrated that action on climate change is not only necessary but also attractive, and refers readers to the forthcoming Climate Bill. With respect to Eddington, the lesson learned by government is that new cross-country links are not needed, but that targeted investment can produce attractive returns.

The government has set twin major goals, with the economy coming first. The transport system should maximise the competitiveness and productivity of the economy, through effectively using existing networks, making target investments and delivering improvements more effectively by improving decision making, speeding approval and reforming planning. The second transport goal is to deal with climate change, by putting a price on carbon, by investing in Research and Development and by removing barriers by improving urban design and providing good public transport. Three further goals are proposed: safety, security and health, improved quality of life and improved equality of opportunity.

While the paper is positioned as the integration of *The Stern Review* and *The Eddington Study* with respect to transport, it is notable that the economy comes first, and that the presumption remains that transport helps the economy by promoting mobility. From this set of assumptions it is but a short step to the policy directives, which seem primarily aimed at managing the existing system more effectively, and making targeted investments in adding capacity on the national network—including Crossrail, Thameslink and new railway carriages.

At the level of urban networks, the government proposes new evaluation tools that will accompany regional funding, with the emphasis on bus stations, guided bus and tram, local road schemes and traffic management. Incentive funding to encourage the adoption of pricing regimes is proposed, along with an emphasis on travel behaviour change and education programmes to encourage greener modes and more sustainable school travel. The paper also proposes that the Department for Transport will work with Communities and Local Government to ensure that new homes and 'eco towns' are located on transport networks, but doesn't suggest that new network capacity should be provided—railway stations, trams or guided buses—at places where major urban extensions or new communities are to be built. There is no proposal to dramatically expand public transport networks in cities outside London or to achieve a quantum level of change in walking and cycling through investment and urban design.

In fact, rather than favouring the green modes, the new plan for a Sustainable Transport System endorses the "mode neutral" approach proposed by Sir Rod Eddington, suggesting that investments in public transport, walking or cycling should only be undertaken if the economic benefits—once 'externalities' are included—justify them over road or traffic management alternatives. The cost-benefit analyses proposed do not at this point appear to take into account the ability of public transport investments to support enhanced density, for example.

While pricing is cited throughout as key to changing behaviour, the commitment to pricing and congestion charging is only to offer incentive grants to local authorities to undertake pilot schemes, leaving the political challenge to local councillors.

For the long term, the paper proposes a detailed process to set measurable objectives, take input, establish evaluation methods and generate and evaluate options, all leading to a long-term plan to be adopted in 2012. For the period to 2012, the framework outlined above, which largely relies upon existing commitments, will be used.

In summary, then, the paper *Towards a Sustainable Transport System* concludes the following:

- It is possible to have a strong economy and address climate change and other goals in transport policy.

- The transport network does not need fundamental reform, and the right connections are largely in place. "Grand projects" are generally not needed.

- A more robust and complex process for evaluating costs and benefits of transport projects is the fundamental change needed, and such an evaluation scheme should account for externalities and be mode neutral.

- Road pricing is key to changing behaviour and should be implemented by local authorities. The government's role should be limited to providing incentive grants for pilot projects.

- Most of the right commitments are in place, but by 2012 a new long-range plan should be adopted. Many of these commitments include schemes to add capacity to the motorway system.

In the next chapter I will present a case study from work The Prince's Foundation has done with the London Borough of Waltham Forest to try to demonstrate the impact of a coordinated approach, linking planning for growth, public transport provision, and provision for walking and travel behaviour change. Hopefully, this will support the argument that a more fundamental change in thinking is needed and that a new kind of networked approach is required: one which looks at walking, cycling public transport and sustainable communities as a single network, and one which replaces the transport idea of providing mobility with a community goal of providing accessibility. In this context it is clear that we are still waiting for the fundamental shift in transport thinking that is necessary to take us toward our vision for 2025.

CASE STUDY—AN OUTER LONDON TOWN CENTRE GROWS UP

In 2007, the London Borough of Waltham Forest and The Prince's Foundation for the Built Environment entered into an agreement to work together to craft a new vision for Walthamstow town centre.

The Borough was concerned about competition from other outer London centres, especially Stratford City, and their impact upon the retail offer in the town centre. Housing stock in Walthamstow was under increasing pressure, with its predominantly two-storey Victorian stock being rapidly converted into flats. At the same time, the London plan was calling for increases in housing and for reductions in carbon emissions, largely due to Walthamstow's high level of accessibility. Local residents were concerned about the pace of change, about the reduction in family accommodation, the prospect of new high-density high-rise flats and about the quality of the retail offer.

In order to address these concerns the two parties agreed to undertake an Enquiry by Design for the Walthamstow town centre in order to engage stakeholders in the creation of a holistic vision and action plan for the area. With support from the London Development Authority, the goals for the two step effort were to increase housing supply, improve the retail offer and offer employment opportunities in Walthamstow centre, while addressing community concerns and taking advantage of public transport accessibility to create a low carbon walkable eco-centre. The Prince's Foundation used an urban design technique called Enquiry by Design, which it had pioneered with English Partnerships for the creation of Sustainable Urban Extensions at Upton in Northampton, Aldershot Barracks and Telford, and adapted this technique to fit the emerging requirements of the new planning system. This required a multi-stage process, with the generation of options with stakeholders, the testing of these options through a formal consultation effort, and the refinement of these options into a preferred option through a second stage of an Enquiry by Design in order to reflect community input.

The entire planning effort took place in Walthamstow at a church hall, allowing continuing attendance from Council staff, local business people and members of the public. A formal consultation was undertaken by Renaisi on the results of the design workshops and resulted in the engagement of both active and hard-to-reach constituencies, and resulted in the selection of a preferred option. As part of the process the Foundation engaged the support of an American NGO called the Centre for Neighbourhood Technologies, to advise on both implementation mechanism and to build a data base for assessing the climate impacts of changes in built form. Space Syntax studied connectivity issues and Alan Baxter Associates analysed transport issues. Another American firm, Seth Harry and Associates led the design and engagement effort to look at the future of the Selbourne Walk enclosed shopping mall.

Enquiry by Design: What is it?
The Enquiry by Design (EbD) process brings together the key stakeholders in a proposed development—statutory agencies and authorities, landowners, the local community, voluntary groups and representatives of employers and retailers—to collaborate in articulating a vision for a site through an intensive workshop, facilitated by a multi-disciplinary design team.

Current government policy sees the effective engagement and participation of local people, local groups and businesses in the planning and design of their communities as a crucial component in making successful places in which people want to live and work and which will stand the test of time.

Enquiry by Design, by bringing together everyone with knowledge about, or interest in, a place to create a new vision, implements this essential collective approach. Enquiry by Design is not just a means of informing the community about a planned development but actively engages them in the planning and design of their community, helping to build up the confidence and collective enthusiasm to allow the vision to be taken forward after the workshop has been completed.

The EbD workshop is an intense process which routinely produces innovative and dynamic solutions to key issues. Such success is attainable because all key decision makers, stakeholders and those with technical expertise are together in the same room; problems are discussed and resolved as and when they arise.

Enquiry by Design shares similarities with other types of planning workshops. However, the difference lies in the degree of technical input; fundamental to the EbD process is the intensive design enquiry within which every issue and possible solution is tested by being drawn, and is presented to the rest of the group for comment and analysis.

The Enquiry by Design seeks the involvement and comment of everyone in the local community and as such, offers the chance to all interest groups to engage with the process and find representation for their voice through it, albeit to varying degrees. The number of days for an EbD can vary, and by its very nature there can be no such thing as a 'generic EbD' since every site is different, however it is normal for an Enquiry by Design to run for five working days. The unique and inclusive nature of the process makes a quick delivery plan far more achievable than seeking out the more conventional planning routes. By the end of the fifth day, at the close of the EbD, the product of the week is a vision for the site which is shared by everyone who is linked to the development, including those responsible for granting the planning permission. This makes a quick delivery of the plan more achievable in a shorter space of time.

The climate analysis built upon work undertaken by a team in which participated in the US in the 1990s, in collaboration with the Centre for Neighbourhood Technology and the Natural Resources Defense Council, with funding from the US Environmental Protection Administration and the Federal Transit Administration, during the Clinton-Gore Administration. The research effort, led by physicist John Holtzclaw, looked at travel patterns at the neighbourhood scale by examining millions of data records for auto ownership and use at the neighborhood level in three metropolitan areas (the San Francisco Bay Area, the Chicago region, and Southern California). Researchers analysed a number of factors including income, household size, net residential density, transit accessibility, quality of the pedestrian environment and existence of neighborhood retail, and developed an algorithm for predicting auto ownership and use and household transportation expenditures. The study found that, "observed differences in density and transit can explain over 3:1 variations in vehicle miles driven per household for a constant level of income and household".[20] This relationship is depicted below.

20 Holtzclaw, John, Robert Clear, Hank Dittmar, David Goldstein and Peter Haas, "Location Efficiency: Neighborhood and Socioeconomic Characteristics Determine Auto Ownership and Use", *Transportation Planning and Technology* (Vol. 25:2002), p. 35.

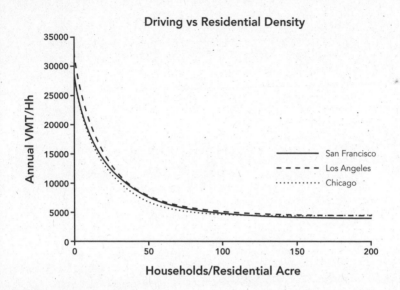

The key variables for measuring location efficiency, once household size and income were controlled for, were found to be:

- Households per residential acre.

- Zonal transit density, which combines transit service frequency and proximity to the stop or station.

- Pedestrian/bicycle friendliness, which measures street grid, age of housing and bonuses for traffic calming measures.[21]

21 Holtzclaw, John, et al, pp. 8–10

The research has profound implications for climate protection, for when one maps these relationships in terms of vehicle travel as carbon emissions from household travel; it becomes clear that urban form is key to climate mitigation. The following chart prepared by some colleagues of mine at the Centre for Neighbourhood Technology, a Chicago based think tank, for a project on transport and climate change, makes the point quite clearly. The chart depicts greenhouse gas emissions for the Chicago region on per square mile basis, making cities look far dirtier than the suburbs and farmland. But when one recalculates on a per capita basis, a very different story emerges: on a per capita basis, city centres contribute much less carbon to the atmosphere than do suburban areas.

These characteristics add up to something called "location efficiency". Location efficiency, which can be quantified, is the combination of greater residential density, increased pedestrian and bicycle friendliness and access to public transport. Improved location efficiency results in reduced vehicle travel, lower carbon emissions and reduced household transportation expenses.

The Prince's Foundation effort at Walthamstow sought to develop similar information for London, and to build a tool to allow local authorities and urban designers to calculate the climate impact of changes in urban form. As a first step, and with the assistance of Transport for London, the CNT researchers collected data on vehicle ownership and use, residential density and transport system characteristics and use.

The model was built using a multi-dimensional linear regression analysis of the London metropolitan area. Vehicle ownership and driving distances are modelled separately. Both geographies are defined by the National Statistics; however, given the sample size of the Transport for London LTDS, it was necessary to use a larger geography to model distances.

Two Views of cities and CO$_2$

Centre for Neighbourhood Technology

CO$_2$ Generated by Automobiles in the Chicago Region per Year

Traditional View:

Cities produce large amounts of GHGs.

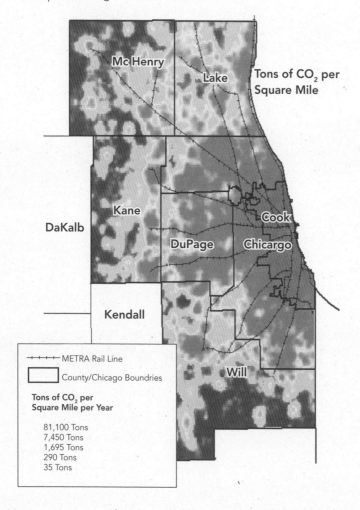

Tons of CO$_2$ per Square Mile

McHenry

Lake

Kane

DaKalb

Cook

DuPage

Chicargo

Kendall

Will

+++++ METRA Rail Line

County/Chicago Boundries

Tons of CO$_2$ per
Square Mile per Year

81,100 Tons
7,450 Tons
1,695 Tons
290 Tons
35 Tons

Emerging View:
City dwellers produce relatively low amounts of GHGs.

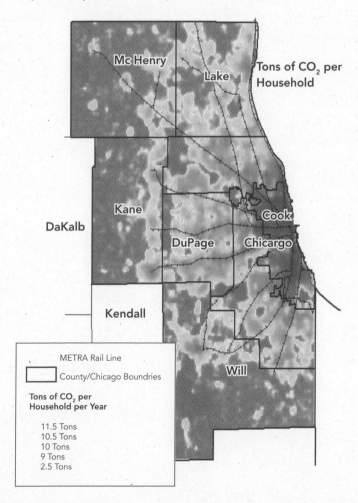

Tons of CO_2 per Household

Mc Henry

Lake

DaKalb

Kane

DuPage

Cook

Chicargo

Kendall

Will

METRA Rail Line

County/Chicago Boundries

Tons of CO_2 per
Household per Year

11.5 Tons
10.5 Tons
10 Tons
9 Tons
2.5 Tons

The Location Efficiency model utilises nine independent variables. Six of these variables are categorised as built environment and three are categorised as household characteristics. The built environment variables reference the actual characteristics of a place and include household density (both net and total), vehicle travel distance, job density, percentage transit, and road concentration. Percentage of public transport users is used to measure access to fixed rail or readily available bus service. The road concentration variable is used as a proxy to measure walkability, as more roads typically implies a grid street network that yields more walking and bicycle opportunities. The household

variables are workers per household, size of household, and an income indicator for distressed communities.

To calculate vehicle ownership the independent variables are regressed against the dependant variable of auto ownership collected by National Statistics. To calculate the driving distances the independent variables are regressed against the dependant variable of annual driving distances derived from the Transport for London LTDS.

Splitting the household and built environment variables apart allows measurement of the impact of the built environment versus household characteristics, as well as to enable

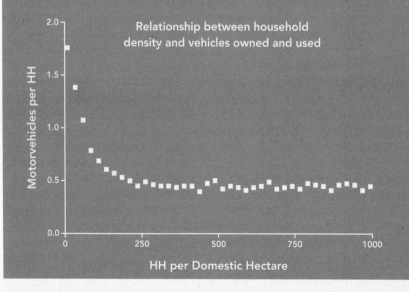

Relationship between household density and vehicles owned and used

inputs of any of the variables to reflect potential changes. The chart below depicts the relationship between vehicle ownership and residential density in London.

The chart clearly shows that as density increased from suburban density levels to more urban densities approaching 50 households per hectare—which is the average density required by London planners—vehicle ownership declines.

The same relationship was found with respect to vehicle travel: that as residential density increases in London, vehicle travel declines. The curve flattens as one gets to hyper densities. The study clearly demonstrated that the location efficiency effects were found in London as well as in the US.

As a final step in building the model, the researchers mapped carbon emissions from driving across London, to analyse whether carbon emissions declines with increases in residential density. They found that annual CO_2 per household produced from driving is markedly less in areas with location efficient qualities. This measure increases considerably the further from central London one travels. These findings are consistent with the urban patterns found within US cities, where compact location efficient neighbourhoods allow households to own fewer vehicles and drive less.

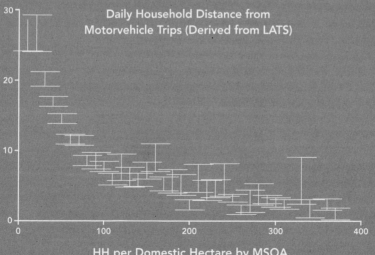

Daily Household Distance from Motorvehicle Trips (Derived from LATS)

HH per Domestic Hectare by MSOA

CO$_2$ From Auto Use in Greater London:
City Dwellers Produce Less GHGs per Household

N

0   5   10
kilometers

Applying Location
Efficiency to Walthamstow
Town Centre

Based on the London Area Transportation Survey for 2001, which only measures the direct distance of any trip not the actual distance driven and for only a small sample of households. Assuming this sampled distance represents the average distance driven by households in the MSOA. That distance is scaled so that the average annual VKT per HH for Greater London is 17,160 KM/year. This auto use is then scaled by an emission factor of 180 grams CO_2/km.

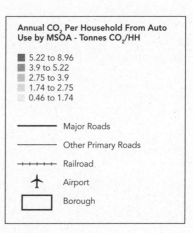

Annual CO_2 Per Household From Auto Use by MSOA - Tonnes CO_2/HH

- 5.22 to 8.96
- 3.9 to 5.22
- 2.75 to 3.9
- 1.74 to 2.75
- 0.46 to 1.74

—————— Major Roads

—————— Other Primary Roads

+++++++ Railroad

✈ Airport

☐ Borough

Walthamstow Town Centre—Masterplan Option B

1 - 2 Storeys
3 - 4 Storeys
5 - 7 Storeys
8 Storeys and above

100 m

Armed with this information, The Prince's Foundation and
The Waltham Forest team undertook its effort to master-plan
Walthamstow Town Centre. The first Enquiry by Design workshop
produced three options: a status quo option in which developers
and the local authority responded in a reactive fashion to one
another, a market orientated option, in which development was
largely driven by developer and landowner preferences, and a
sustainable development option which balanced London plan
objectives with qualities identified as essential to Walthamstow by
community residents.

The two key options were Options B and C, with Option B
reflecting the developer preference for opportunistic intervention
at key parcels, as well as the current preference in the industry for
the construction of one and two bedroom flats in tower buildings
for the buy-to-let market. The master-plan and massing diagram for
Option B is depicted on the previous page.

Option C was an attempt to reflect community preferences,
London plan goals and national policy, as well as the market
demands, in an integrated fashion. Instead of towers, an attempt
was made to increase density by developing a connected set
of blocks replacing the parking lots and industrial land in South
Grove and then, over time, phasing out one-storey shopping
malls and building a multi-storey retail-led mixed-use complex.
Heights reflected heights found in denser parts of London such
as Kensington and Chelsea and Swiss Cottage, where four-and
five-storey terraces and six- and seven-storey mansion blocks
predominate, reflecting a precedent analysis which found that
these areas accommodated significantly higher numbers of
dwelling units within a 400 metre radius of the transport hubs
than did Walthamstow Town Centre. The Option C plan shown
overleaf accommodates over 2,500 dwelling units.

In 2007, The second phase Enquiry by Design was held, with the
goal of using community input to craft a more detailed preferred
option for acceptance by Councillors and further public input in

the autumn. The public input was overwhelmingly in support of
Option C, with 52 per cent favouring Option C and only 20 per
cent favouring Option B, although members of the community
and other stakeholders favoured aspects of all options.

The Enquiry by Design was a five day exercise culminating
in a preferred option, which called for improved walking
connections through the Town Centre, the retention and
realignment of the popular outdoor market, the development
of a new mixed-use neighbourhood on largely vacant
and underutilised land at South Grove, and the phased
redevelopment of the single-storey city centre shopping mall
into a connected, lively multi-storey mixed-use centre with
retail at the ground floor and employment and residential
uses above. Over 2,400 housing units were provided, with
a large amount being three and four bedroom units, and all
being accommodated either in three-to four-storey terraces
with gardens or five-to seven-storey mansion blocks with
internal courtyards. Residential density per hectare in the
Town Centre will be increased under the plan.

The resulting final master-plan, which was adopted by
the Council as its preferred option for a second round of
consultation, is depicted on pages 56 and 57.

Heights are limited to seven storeys throughout, and the
master-plan provides for significant retail including a large
food store, for improvement of the street market, improved
pedestrian and bus connections to and through the centre,
as well as for employment land uses. A school, play areas
and open space were also provided and a Town Centre
business improvement district was proposed both to manage
the public realm and to oversee environmental issues
including the implementation of travel behaviour plans for
new development and integration with provisions of the
London Climate Change Action Plan for improving the energy
performance of existing buildings.

Walthamstow Town Centre—Masterplan Option C

1 - 2 Storeys
3 - 4 Storeys
5 - 7 Storeys

100 m

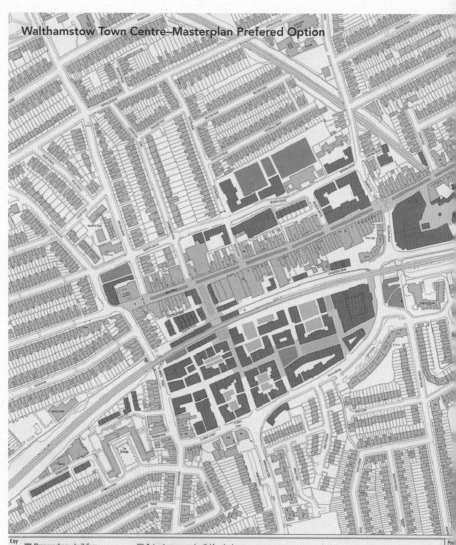

Walthamstow Town Centre–Masterplan Prefered Option

Key
- Proposed new buildings
- Existing buildings
- Green space - public
- Green space - private
- School green - potential for dual use
- Key public open spaces
- Squares - hard surface
- Improved market stalls

WALTHAMSTOW
25th MAY 2007 EbD

TOWN PLAN

Scale size			
1:2500@A2			
Drawn		Checked	
-			
Client		Date	
WALTHAM FOREST		10.08.2007	

0 25 50 100m

THIS DRAWING MAY BE USED ONLY FOR THE
PURPOSE INTENDED AND ONLY WRITTEN
DIMENSIONS SHALL BE USED

The Prince's Foundation

19-22 Charlotte Road
London, EC2A 3SG
Tel: 0207 613 8500
Fax: 0207 613 8599
enquiry@princes-foundation.org
www.princes-foundation.org

The Prince's Foundation

Drawing number	Rev
074-I/11.1101	-

Walthamstow Town Centre Case Study

An analysis was performed of the impact on carbon emissions as against outer London average densities using the London location efficiency model. The results of the analysis were significant, finding annual reductions of three tonnes of carbon per household.

Efficient Communities Reduce GHG Emissions

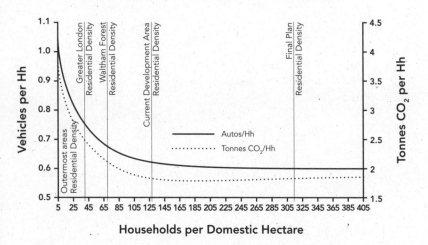

Households per Domestic Hectare

The next steps with this model will involve the development of quick response forecasting tools to test various scenarios for development, incorporation of finer grained travel data, as well as building a module which looks at both housing and transport costs on a local area basis to assess affordability impacts alongside climate impacts, for a more integrated picture of sustainability.

The Walthamstow case has much to tell about reforming transport policy in this country, as it demonstrates four key points:

- The linkage of public transport access and new development through transport-orientated development can be a powerful weapon in the climate change campaign;

- There is considerable opportunity to develop near existing transport capacity as a way of meeting development goals sustainably, if this is undertaken in concert with improuved walkability.

- Mid-rise development densities can achieve needed climate and housing impacts without disrupting existing neighbourhoods and destroying their character and liveability. One can have greater density and family housing.

- A next generation of transport thinking that views communities, walkability and public transport as a single green network can help to resolve the conflict between the economy and the environment that plagues policy makers.

TOWARDS THE SUSTAINABLE CITY:
POLICY AND IMPLEMENTATION

Despite the urgent need for transport policy that addresses sustainability issues, government seems to be pursuing an incremental approach: addressing capacity issues without even meeting forecast demand on the railway.

It appears that while the Department for Transport abandoned the "predict and provide" approach over a decade ago, the policy they have put in place instead is one of "predict and then don't provide", as recent capacity increases on the railway network don't even keep up with current or forecast increases in ridership. Instead the Department proposes a multi-year evaluation process, in which all ideas are individually scrutinised through a lens of cost-benefit analysis, and only those with high scores are pursued.

Network effects and synergies seem to be ignored, as is the notion of a set of reinforcing policies and practices, all sacrificed upon the altar of better and more rigorous economic evaluation.

It is clear that incrementalism of the sort proposed by Sir Rod Eddington derives from the proposition that the UK is basically on the right track with respect to transport. If one does not believe that this is the case, then a different end state must be visualised, and then steps taken to move toward that end state. A new approach would begin with a set of new assumptions, which would help to define a set of linked policies and investments. These underlying principles can be described as follows:

- Sustainable transport requires a sustainable city, and this implies a linking of transport policy and investments with planning and development.

- Sustainable cities rely upon accessibility, rather than mobility, reducing the need to travel by car, particularly for local trips. This implies a city of short distances, and also implies increasing blurring of the boundaries between information networks and physical networks, so that trip substitution becomes a norm rather than an exception.

- An emphasis on accessibility means that Gross Domestic Product is not seen as being linked to growth in personal motorvehicle travel.

- Transport is a public utility, and the passenger transport system must be viewed and managed as a coordinated network: reasonable levels of public transport accessibility must be provided.

- Provision of sustainable transport infrastructure, especially fixed guideway systems such as streetcar, tram, guided busway and railway stations, will increase accessibility and drive up land value. Mechanisms that capture this increased land value can help to fund the infrastructure.

- The walkable mixed-use neighbourhood is the foundation of the sustainable city, and of a successful public transport system.

- Market based strategies including road pricing are essential, but not sufficient: they must be accompanied by investments in new public transport coordinated with development orientated to it and by programs to support changes in travel behaviour. Vehicle technology is an essential fix, but not the long-term solution. Travel behaviour change programmes are essential components of a strategy of mutually reinforcing and synergistic measures.

- The scale of the problem demands immediate solutions, and technology fixes, while attractive cannot deliver in the short-term. Relying upon technology is very high-risk, as the lead times are long and the likelihood of payoffs uncertain. By the time we find out a technological fix hasn't worked, further climate change will have happened. For the same reason, we cannot afford to wait for the development of new evaluation tools before we begin to plan for sustainable transport future, as Eddington has proposed.

The policies and investments needed are common sense, and the successes in London's transport policies over the past decade are the surest indication that a coordinated set of reinforcing policies will work. What is needed isn't more analysis: what are required now are leadership, investment and coordination.

In his recent book *Unsustainable Transport*, Professor David Banister, who heads the Transport Studies Unit at Oxford University, described the sustainable city:

> The city is the most sustainable urban form and it has to form the location where most (70–80 per cent) of the world's population will live. The key parameters of the city are that it should be over 25,000 population

(preferably over 50,000), with medium densities (over 40 persons per hectare), with mixed-use developments, and with preference given to developments in public transport accessible corridors and near to highly public transport accessible interchanges. Such developments conform to the requirements of service and information based economies. Settlements of this scale would also be linked together to form agglomerations of polycentric cities, with clear hierarchies that would allow a close proximity of everyday facilities and accessibility to higher order activities.

The intention is not to prohibit the use of the car as this would be both difficult to achieve and it would be seen as being against notions of freedom and choice. The intention is to design cities of such quality and at a suitable scale that people would not need to have a car and they would choose to live in a car free location.[22]

22 Banister, David, *Unsustainable Transport: City Transport in the New Century*, London: Spon, 2005

Daily life in this sustainable city was described in the first chapter. What are needed are a linked set of policies and investments to take us toward this clear vision. Such a linked set of policies must promote not only greener travel modes such as public transport and cycling, but also the reduction of the need to travel through the area of many of one's daily needs within walking distance and trip substitution through telecommuting. The city must be viewed in network terms, with neighbourhoods being viewed as both liveable places and as nodes in a metropolitan public transportation network. The linking of node and place, defined by European researchers Luca Bertolini and Tejo Spit in their book *Cities on Rails*, is the way that we will reconcile local identity and character with a global economy in the sustainable twenty-first century city.[23]

23 Bertolini, L and T Spit, *Cities on Rails. The Redevelopment of Railway Station Areas*, London and New York: Spon/ Routledge, 1998

This notion of integrating development with public transport interchanges is called transit-oriented development in the US, and a body of scholarship has grown up to document the economic and travel reduction benefits of directing growth toward railway and busway interchange points, including a book edited by myself and Gloria Ohland, *The New Transit Town: Best Practises in Transit Oriented Development.* Like many of the other policy proposals contained herein, it is simply common sense, and reflects development patterns evident through England as our cities grew up around railway and public transport stops.

This networked approach will require a comprehensive set of policies across government, involving both its departements for Communities and Local Government and Transport, and requiring planning support at the level of the regions as well.

To reach a sustainable transport vision by 2025, a set of actions is needed now, including:

- Linking transport and growth, so that no new housing is permitted that is not within 800 metres of public transport and within 800 metres of a shop. New communities or eco-towns must be located at major public transport hubs, and related to regional employment concentrations in a conurbation, and built around the concept of walkable neighbourhoods.

- The concept of "community infrastructure levies" being proposed by the government to replace the Section 106 agreements should be extended to allow partial funding of sustainable transport infrastructure and sustainable drainage under a theory of value capture, including tram systems, rapid bus systems, rail stations and transport interchanges and facilities for cycling and walking.

- Carbon taxes and road pricing should be adopted, not for the sole purpose of lessening congestion but for the purpose of supporting the shift to greener travel modes and a reduction in the need to travel, through land use strategies and travel behaviour change programmes.

- Programmes to reduce the energy consumption of rail, bus and tram should be undertaken along with programmes to regulate fuel economy; both through vehicle technology fixes and changes in driving behaviour.

- The growth in rail travel should be continued, with expansion of high-speed rail systems from Europe into the UK, including both a north-south high-speed link from St Pancras and a service from London to the West. In 2004, the Commission for Integrated Transport recommended that government begin planning for a high-speed rail network, warning that the alternative was "higher fares which would be both unfair and drive passengers back on to an already crowded roads network". The Commission noted that there was scope for considerable savings in costs, which if implemented could result in benefits outweighing costs by three to one.[24]

24 Commission for Integrated Transport, "Planning for High Speed Rail Needed Now", September 2004, viewed at http://www.cfit. gov.uk/pn/040209/ index.htm

- Public transport links to outer London stations should be considered to relieve bottlenecks coming into central London, and incremental improvements in speed and capacity should be continued, along with major investments in stations.

- Not only London but also all of the UK's major cities must be viewed as polycentric metropolitan areas, and as the hubs of economic regions, and land use-transport visions should be developed for all of them, employing the backcasting approach used herein. Such regional strategies eschew the predict and provide plans of the past to engage communities in deciding what future they want for themselves and then identifying the policy package necessary to achieve that future. Peter Calthorpe and William Fulton described this approach in their 2003 book *The Regional City*, and Calthorpe and colleague

John Fregonese have undertaken these kinds of sustainability plans for Chicago, Southern California, Portland, Oregon, Louisiana and Austin, Texas in the US.[25]

- Strategies to improve the walkability of existing neighbourhoods and introduce mixed-use should be implemented alongside programmes to retrofit existing buildings for energy efficiency. It is essential to reduce carbon emissions from both buildings and transport.

- Travel behaviour changes, already being piloted by government, should accompany all new commercial and residential development, with introductory information and public transport discount packages provided to new employees and incoming residents alike. Studies have shown that the most effective interventions in travel behaviour occur immediately after relocation. Such programmes can be mandated as part of planning approval, and administered by Business Improvement Districts (BIDs), housing associations and community benefit corporations set up to manage new developments.

- The greenest travel modes are walking, cycling and avoiding travel altogether, and programmes need to be in place for these modes too. As Eddington notes, often the smaller programmes can have high payoffs, and the creation of continuous cycle networks, interconnected walkable streets, and the encouragement of flexible working, job sharing, and satellite and home-working all will play a major part in this change toward a networked, sustainable city.

Adding it all up: Getting to 2025

The idea of a networked approach and that set of synergistic policies imply that there is an additive effect: that one plus one might truly equal three. Evidence to this effect was provided by a recent study that took the backcasting approach employed here. The study, undertaken by Robin Hickman and the aforementioned

25 Calthorpe, Peter and William Fulton, *The Regional City: Planning for the End of Sprawl*, Washington, DC: Island Press, 2003

David Banister, looked at two alternative policy packages, and their ability to meet a 60 per cent CO_2 reduction by 2025. The policy packages included one called "New Market Economy" focused on market forces and technology breakthroughs, and one focused upon "Smart Social Policy" which emphasised public transport, walking, cycling and behaviour change. 122 measures were analysed, and then assembled into policy packages that were mutually reinforcing. The analysis revealed that the market/technology scenario could not deliver the required reduction of emissions, but that "the 60 per cent CO_2 reduction target in 2025 can be achieved by a combination of strong behavioural change and strong technological innovation. But it is in travel behaviour that the real breakthrough must take place and this should be implemented now."[26]

26 Hickman, R and David, Banister, "Looking over the horizon, Transport and reduced CO_2 emissions in the UK by 2025", Transport Policy 14, 2007, pp. 377–387

There are a series of stark choices ahead of us. As the evidence about climate change mounts, it has become ever clearer that the time for action is now. Yet lack of funding and a paralysis of analysis have led to a point where the approach being taken to transport is to allow road transport real costs to continue to decline while studying the alternative, while the public transport costs rise and the system becomes intolerably more crowded. Common sense would dictate dramatic improvements to the overtaxed networks for rail, public transport and cycling funded from road pricing or carbon taxes, yet common sense is sacrificed upon the altar of cost benefit analysis and fear of driver backlash.

What is needed is courage and leadership, and a clear statement of vision for where we want to get to by 2025. As we have seen, the vision for 2025 is one in which quality of life is improved rather than degraded, and the changes are ones which can improve one's interactions with family, with colleagues and with community. The alternative can also be clearly seen: crowded roads and trains, longer commutes, and higher costs to fix the problem if we fail to act.

SUGGESTING READING

General

"Barker Review of Land Use Planning", Department of Communities and Local Government, 2006.

Florida, Richard, *The Rise of the Creative Class*, London: Basic Books, 2002.

Foxell Simon, ed., *The professionals' choice: The future of the built environment professions*, London: Building Futures, 2003.

Kunstler, James Howard, *The Long Emergency*, Atlantic Monthly Press, 2005.

Leadbeater, Charles, *Personalisation through participation: A new script for public services*, London: Demos, 2004.

Schumacher, EF, *Small is Beautiful*, Vancouver: Hartley & Marks,1999.

Economic Survey of the United Kingdom, OECD, 2007.
World Population Prospects: The 2006 Revision, Population Division of the Department of Economic and Social Affairs of the United Nations Secretariat, United Nations, 2007.

Planet Earth and Climate Change

Flannery, Tim, *The Weather Makers: The History and Future Impact of Climate Change*, Melbourne: Text Publishing, 2005.

Gore, Al, *Earth in the Balance: Ecology and the Human Spirit*, Boston: Houghton Mifflin, 1992.

Gore, Al, *The Assault on Reason*, Harmondsworth: Penguin, 2007.

Hartmann, Thom, *Last Hours of Ancient Sunlight*, New York: Three Rivers Press, 1997 (rev. 2004).

Hawken, Lovins & Lovins, *Natural Capitalism*, London: Little Brown, 1999.

Hillman, Mayer, *How We Can Save the Planet*, Harmondsworth: Penguin, 2004.

Homer-Dixon, Thomas, *The Upside of Down: Catastrophe, Creativity and the Renewal of Civilisation*, New York: Alfred A Knopf, 2006.

Kolbert, Elizabeth, *Field Notes from a Catastrophe: A Frontline Report on Climate Change*, London: Bloomsbury, 2006.

Lovelock, James, *Gaia: A New Look at Life on Earth*, Oxford: Oxford University Press, 1979.

Lovelock, James, *The Revenge of Gaia*, London: Allen Lane, 2006.

Lynas, Mark, *High Tide: The Truth About Our Climate Crisis*, London: Picador, 2004.

Lynas, Mark, *Six Degrees: Our Future on a Hotter Planet*, London: Fourth Estate, 2007.

Marshall, George, *Carbon Detox*, London: Gaia Thinking, 2007.

McDonough, W, and Braungert M, *Cradle to Cradle, Remaking the Way*

We Make Things, New York: North Point Press, 2002.

Monbiot, George, *Heat: How We Can Stop the Planet Burning*, London: Allen Lane, 2006.

Walker, G, and King D, *The Hot Topic: How to Tackle Global Warming and Still Keep the Lights On*, London: Bloomsbury, 2008.

Action Today to Protect Tomorrow—The Mayor's Climate Change Action Plan, London: GLA, 2007.

Climate Change The UK Programme, London: DEFRA, 2006.

Summary for Policymakers of the Synthesis Report of the IPCC Fourth Assessment Report, United Nations, 2007.

Cities

Girardet, Herbert, *Cities People Planet: Liveable Cities for a Sustainable World*, Chichester: Wiley-Academy, 2004.

Jacobs, Jane, *The Death and Life of Great American Cities*, New York: Random House, 1961.

Jacobs, Jane, *The Economy of Cities*, New York: Random House, 1969.

Mumford, Lewis, *The Culture of Cities*, New York: Secker & Warburg, 1938.

Sudjic, Deyan, "Cities on the edge of chaos", *The Observer*, March 2008.

Urban Task Force, *Towards an Urban Renaissance*, London: E&FN Spon, 1999.

Work

Abramson, Daniel M, *Building the Bank of England*, New Haven, CT: Yale University Press, 2005.

Alexander, Christopher, *The Timeless Way of Building*, Oxford: Oxford University Press, 1979.

Anderson, Ray, *Mid-Course Correction: The Interface Model*, Chelsea Green, 2007.

Brand, Stewart, *How Buildings Learn*, New York: Viking Press, 1994.

Brinkley, Ian, *Defining the Knowledge Economy, Knowledge Economy Programme Report*, London: The Work Foundation, 2006.

Castells, Manuel, *The Information Age: Economy, Society, Culture*, Oxford: Blackwell, 1996.

Davenport, Tom, *Thinking for a Living*, Boston: Harvard Business School Press, 2005.

Dodgson, Gann, and Salter, *Think, Play, Do*, Oxford, 2005.

Dodgson, Gann and Salter, *The management of technological innovation strategy and practice*, Oxford: Oxford University Press, 2008.

Duffy, Francis, *The Changing Workplace*, London: Phaidon, 1992.

Duffy, Francis, *The New Office*, London: Conran Octopus, 1997.

Duffy, Francis, *Architectural Knowledge*, London: E&FN Spon, 1998.

Duffy, Cave, Worthington, *Planning Office Space*, London: The Architectural Press, 1976.

Galloway, L, *Office Management: Its Principles and Practice*, Oxford: The Ronald Press, 1918.

Gann, David, *Building Innovation*, London: Thomas Telford, 2000.

Giedion, Siegfried, *Mechanization Takes Command*, Oxford: Oxford University Press, 1948.

Gilbreth, FB, *Motion Study*, New York: Van Nostrand, 1911. .

Gottfried, David, *Greed to Green*, Berkeley, CA: Worldbuild Publishing, 2004.

Groak, Steven, *Is Construction an Industry?*, Construction Management and Economics, 1994.

Handy, Charles, *Understanding Organizations*, Harmondsworth: Penguin, 1967.

Hawken, Paul, *The Ecology of Commerce*, New York: HarperCollins, 1993.

Mitchell, William J, *City of Bits*, Cambridge, MA: MIT Press, 1995.

Quinan, Jack, *Frank Lloyd Wright's Larkin Building*, Cambridge, MA: MIT Press, 1987.

Sassen, Saskia, *A Sociology of Globalization*, New York: Norton, 2006.

Sennett, Richard, *The Culture of the New Capitalism*, New Haven, CT: Yale University Press, 2006.

Taylor, Frederick, *The Principles of Scientific Management*, New York: Harper & Brothers, 1911.

Trease, Geoffrey, *Samuel Pepys and His World*, London: Thames and Hudson, 1972.

Education

Aston and Bekhradnia, *Demand for Graduates: A review of the economic evidence*, Higher Education Policy Institute, 2003.

Friere, Paolo, *Education: the practice of freedom*, London: Writers and Readers Cooperative, 1974.

Gardner, Howard, *Multiple Intelligences*, New York: Basic Books, 1993.

Goodman, Paul, *Growing up absurd*, New York: First Sphere Books, 1970.

Illich, Ivan, *Deschooling Society*, London: Calder and Boyars.1971.

Kimber, Mike, Does Size Matter? *Distributed leadership in small secondary schools*, National College for School Leadership, 2003.

Nair and Fielding, *The Language of School Design*, DesignShare, 2005.

Neil, AS, Summerhill, Harmondsworth: Penguin Books,1968. *The Children's Plan—Building Brighter Futures*, DCSF, December 2007.

Every Child Matters: Change for Children, DfES/HM Government, 2004.

Higher Standards, Better Schools For All, DfES.

2020 Vision Report of the Teaching and Learning in 2020, Review Group, 2006.

www.smallschools.org.uk

www.thecademy.net/
inclusiontrust.org/
Welcome.html

www.eco-schools.org.uk

www.standards.dfes.gov.uk/
personalisedlearning/about/

Transport and Neighbourhoods

Banister, David, *Unsustainable Transport: City Transport in the New Century*, London: E&FN Spon, 2005.

Bertolini L, and T, Spit, *Cities on Rails. The Redevelopment of Railway Station Areas*, London: Spon/Routledge, 1998.

Calthorpe P, and Fulton, W, *The Regional City: Planning for the End of Sprawl*, Washington, DC: Island Press, 2003.

Dittmar H, and Ohland, G, *The New Transit Town: Best Practices in Transit-Oriented Development*, Washington, DC: Island Press, 2004.

Hickman, R and Banister, D, *Looking over the horizon, Transport and reduced CO_2 emissions in the UK by 2030*, Transport Policy, 2007.

Holtzclaw, Clear, Dittmar, Goldstein and Haas, *Location Efficiency: Neighborhood and Socioeconomic Characteristics Determine Auto Ownership and Use*, Transportation Planning and Technology (Vol. 25) 2002.

Commission for Integrated Transport, Planning for High Speed Rail Needed Now, 2004, viewed at http://www.cfit.gov.uk/pn/040209/index.htm

Regional Transport Statistics, National Statistics and Department for Transport, 2006 Edition.

Energy, Transport and Environment Indicators, Eurostat, 2005 Edition.

Toward a Sustainable Transport system, Department for Transport, 2007.

Eddington Transport Study, HM Treasury & Department for Transport, 2007.

UK Foresight programme, *Tackling Obesities: Future Choices*, The Government Office for Science and Technology, 2007.

Community

Dench G, Gavron K, and Young M, *The New East End: Kinship*, Race and Conflict, London: Profile, 2006.

Jacobs, Jane, *The Death and Life of American Cities*, New York: Modern Library, 1961.

Putnam, Robert, *Bowling Alone: The Collapse and Revival of American Community*, New York: Simon & Schuster, 2000.

Young M, and Willmott, P, *Family and Kinship in East London*, Harmondsworth: Penguin, 1957.

Report Card 7, *Child poverty in perspective: An overview of child well-being in rich countries*, UNICEF Innocenti Research Centre, 2007.

Key Facts for Diverse Communities: Ethnicity and Faith, Greater London Authority, Data Management and Analysis Group, 2007.

www.footprintnetwork.org

www.yourhistoryhere

www.fixmystreet.com

Globalisation

Abbott, C, Rogers, P, Sloboda, J, *Global Responses to Global Threats: Sustainable Security for the 21st Century*, Oxford: The Oxford Research Group, 2006.

Balls E, Healey J and Leslie C, *Evolution and Devolution in England*, New Local Government Network, 2006.

Gladwell, Malcolm, *The Tipping Point: How Little Things Can Make a Big Difference*, London: Little Brown, 2000.

Goldsmith, Edward, "How to Feed People under a Regime of Climate Change", *Ecologist Magazine*, 2004.

Gore, Al, *The Assault on Reason*, London: Bloomsbury, 2007.

Gray, John, *Black Mass: Apocalyptic Religion and the Death of Utopia*, London: Allen Lane, 2007.

Guillebaud, John, *Youthquake: Population, Fertility and Environment in the 21st Century*, Optimum Population Trust, 2007.

Hines, Colin, *Localisation: A Global Manifesto*, London: Earthscan, 2000.

Kagan, Robert, *Of Paradise and Power: America and Europe in the New World Order*, New York: Alfred Knopf, 2003.

Martin, James, *The Meaning of the 21st Century*, London: Transworld, 2007.

Meadows, Meadows, Randers and Behrens, *Limits to Growth*, Club of Rome, 1972.

Nordhaus, T, and M, Shellenberger, *Break Through: From the Death of Environmentalism to the Politics of Possibility*,

Boston: Houghton Mifflin, 2007.

Porritt, Jonathon, *Capitalism: As if the World Matters*, London: Earthscan, 2005.

Roszak, Theodore, *World Beware! American Triumphalism in an Age of Terror*, Toronto: Between the Lines, 2006.

Sachs, W, and T, Santarius *Fair Future: Resource Conflicts, Security and Global Justice*, London: Zed Books, 2005.

Kirkpatrick Sale, *Dwellers in the Land*, New Society Publishers, 1991.

Shrybman, Steven, *A Citizen's Guide to the World Trade Organisation*, Ottawa, Canadian Center for Policy Alternatives, 1999.

Soros, George, *The Age of Fallability: The Consequences of the War on Terror*, Beverly Hills, CA: Phoenix Books, 2006.

Stern, Nicholas, *The Economics of Climate Change: The Stern Review*, Cambridge: Cambridge University Press, 2007.

Stiglitz, Joseph, *Globalization and its Discontents*, New York: Norton, 2002.

Stiglitz, Joseph, *Making Globalization Work*, New York: Norton, 2006.

Wolf, Martin, *Why Globalization Works*, New Haven, CT: Yale University Press, 2005.

Johannesburg Manifesto, Fairness in a Fragile World, Berlin: Heinrich Böll Foundation, 2002.

US Defence Dept, *An Abrupt Climate Change Scenario and It's Implications for US Natural Security*, 2003.

WWF, Living Planet Report, WWF International, 2006.

Further websites

The Edge
www.at-the-edge.org.uk

CABE
www.cabe.org.uk

China Dialogue
www.chinadialogue.net

Global Commons Institute (Contraction and Convergence)
www.gci.org.uk

AUTHORS

Bill Gething

Bill Gething is a partner at the architects Feilden Clegg
Bradley Studios, Chair of the RIBA's Sustainable Futures
group, Visiting Professor of Sustainability at the University
of Bath and Chair of the BRE Sustainability Board. He is a
member of the Edge.

Hank Dittmar

Hank Dittmar is an urban designer and transport expert
with over 25 years experience in England and the United
States. He currently serves as Chief Executive of the Prince's
Foundation for the Built Environment, and is a Distinguished
Research Associate at the Oxford University Centre for the
Environment. He was formally Chairman of the Congress for
the New Urbanism and President of Reconnecting America.
During the 1990s he was appointed by US President Bill
Clinton to the White House Policy Dialogue on Controlling
Greenhouse Gas Emissions from Motor Vehicles and served
as the Chairman of the Metropolitan Working Group of the
President's Council on Sustainable Development. He is the
co-author of the 2004 book *New Transit Town*. The views
expressed herein are his own.

THE EDGE

The Edge is a ginger group and think tank, sponsored by the building industry professions, that seeks to stimulate public interest in policy questions that affect the built environment, and to inform and influence public opinion. It was established in 1996 with support from the Arup Foundation. The Edge is supported by The Carbon Trust.

The Edge organises a regular series of debates and other events intended to advance policy thinking in the built environment sector and among the professional bodies within it. For further details, see www.at-the-edge.org.uk

EDGE FUTURES

Edge Futures is a project initiated by The Edge and Black Dog Publishing. It has only been possible with the active participation of The Edge Committee as well as supporting firms and institutions. Special thanks are due to Adam Poole, Duncan McCorquodale, Frank Duffy, Robin Nicholson, Bill Gething, Chris Twinn, Andy Ford, Mike Murray and Jane Powell as well as to all the individual authors.

The project has been generously sponsored by The Carbon Trust, The Commission for Architecture and the Built Environment (CABE), Ramboll Whitbybird, The Arup Foundation, ProLogis and Construction Skills. Thanks are due to all those bodies and to the support of Karen Germain, Elanor Warwick, Mark Whitby, Ken Hall and Guy Hazlehurst within them.
The Edge is also grateful to Sebastian Macmillan of IDBE in Cambridge for the day we spent developing scenarios there and to Philip Guildford for facilitating the session.

Simon Foxell

Much is already known about the state of the world
15 to 20 years from now. Almost all the buildings and
infrastructure are already in place or in development—we
replace our buildings etc., at a very slow pace. The great
majority of the population who'll be living and working
then, especially in the UK, have already been born and
will have been educated in a school system that is familiar
and predictable. The global population, however, will have
increased from 6.7 billion in July 2007 to approximately 8
billion by 2025.

The climate will have changed, mainly as a result of the
emissions of greenhouse gases of the past 50 and more
years, but not by much. The temperature is predicted to be,
on average, half a degree warmer, as well as varying over a
greater range than at present. But, more significantly it will be
understood to be changing, resulting in a strong feeling of
uncertainty and insecurity. Rainfall will have reduced but will
also become more extreme, i.e. tending to drought or flood.
Resources, whether energy, water or food imports, will be in
shorter supply; partly as a result of climate change but also
due to regulations aimed at preventing the effects of global
warming becoming worse. Transport will be constrained as a
result but other technologies will have greatly improved the
ability to economically communicate.

These changes form the context for this first series of five
Edge Futures books, but it is not their subject: that is the
impact of such changes and other developments on our
daily lives, the economy, social and education services
and the way the world trades and operates. Decision
makers are already being challenged to act and formulate
policy, in the face of the change already apparent in the
years ahead. This set of books highlights how critical and
important planning for the future is going to be. Society
will expect and require policy makers to have thought
ahead and prepared for the best as well as the worst. Edge

Futures offers a series of critical views of events, in the next two decades, that need to be planned for today.

The five books intentionally look at the future from very different viewpoints and perspectives. Each author, or pair of authors, has been asked to address a different sector of society, but there is inevitably a great deal of crossover between them. They do not always agree; but consistency is not the intention; that is to capture a breadth of vision as where we may be in 20 years time.

Jonathon Porritt in *Globalism and Regionalism* examines some of the greatest challenges before the planet, including climate change and demographic growth, and lays down the gauntlet to the authors of the other books. Porritt's diagnosis of the need to establish a new balance between the global and the regional over the years ahead and to achieve a 'Civic Globalisation' has an echo in Geoff Mulgan's call in *Living and Community* for strengthening communities through rethinking local governance and rebuilding a sense of place. Both are—perhaps professionally—optimistic that the climate change is a challenge that we, as a society, can deal with, while not underestimating the change that our society is going to have to undergo to achieve it.

Hank Dittmar, writing in *Transport and Networks* is less than certain, that currently, policies are adequately joined-up to deal with the issues that the recent flurry of major reports from the UK Government has highlighted: "Planning" from Barker, "Climate Change" from Stern and "Transport" from Eddington. He notes Barker's comment that "planning plays a role in the mitigation of and adaptation to climate change, the biggest issue faced across all climate areas" but that she then goes on to dismiss the issue. In its approach to all these reviews, the government has shown that it is more concerned with economic growth and indeed it has already concluded that the transport network needs no further fundamental reform. Dittmar believes otherwise, he calls for immediate solutions to support the development of the accessible, sustainable city.

Simon Foxell in *Education and Creativity* sees an even bumpier ride ahead, with progress only being made as a result of the lurch from crisis to crisis. Such discontinuities, will allow the UK to address many longstanding problems, from the personalisation of education to addressing the increasingly cut-throat international competition in creativity, innovation and skills—but not without a great deal of pain and chaos. Bill Mitchell, in the same volume, outlines a way of reconfiguring educational practice to develop just those skills that successful creativity-based economies are going to require.

In *Working*, Frank Duffy sees the end of road for the classic 'American Taylorist' office and the unsuitability of its counterpart, the European social democratic office. In their place, he proposes a new typology—the networked office—that will make better use of the precious resource that is our existing stock of buildings and allow greater integration into the life of the city. And, it is the city that all the authors come back to as a central and unifying theme—the dominant form of the millennium, the place where the majority of mankind now lives. Perhaps this is because, as Deyan Sudjic, Director of the Design Museum, has written recently; "The future of the city has suddenly become the only subject in town."

It is about the largest social unit that most of us can imagine with any ease and is a constant challenge economically, socially and environmentally. If we can work out what a sustainable city might be like and how to deliver it, then maybe we can sleep easier in our beds, less afraid that the end of civilisation, as we recognise it, may be within our childrens', or our childrens' childrens', lifetime. All the component parts of the Edge Futures studies come together in the city; where the community meets the office buildings, the schools and transport system. The city is the hub of the regional response to world events and needs to become a responsive participant in formulating a way out of policy log-jam.

As this first series of Edge Futures shows, the task is urgent and deeply complex but also not impossible. It is only, assuming that we need to make the transition to a low carbon economy within ten to twenty years, in Geoff Mulgan's words: "extraordinarily challenging by any historic precedent."

© 2008 Black Dog Publishing Limited, London, UK and the authors.
All rights reserved.

10a Acton Street
London WC1X 9NG
T. +44 (0)20 7613 1922
F. +44 (0)20 7613 1944
E. info@blackdogonline.com
W. www.blackdogonline.com

Designed by Draught Associates

All opinions expressed within this publication are those of the authors and
not necessarily of the publisher.

British Library Cataloguing-in-Publication Data.
A CIP record for this book is available from the British Library.
ISBN: 978 1 906155 117

Black Dog Publishing, London, UK is an environmentally responsible
company. Edge Futures are printed on Cyclus Offset, a paper produced
from 100% post consumer waste.

architecture art design
fashion history photography
theory and things

black dog
publishing

www.blackdogonline.com